New Zealand Fact Fiesta

"Mind-Blowing Fun Facts That Will Amaze You!"

Bandana Ojha

Introduction

Filled with up-to-date information, fascinating & fun facts this book " New Zealand Fact Fiesta" : "Mind-Blowing Fun Facts That Will Amaze You!" is the best book for kids to find out more about**Land of the Long White Cloud".** This book would satisfy the children's curiosity and help them to understand why New Zealand attracts millions of visitors annually and what makes it different from other countries. This book gives a story, history & explores the country's best cuisine, architecture, fashion, art, language, people, places, national symbols, and many more. It is a fun and fascinating way for young readers to find out more interesting facts. This is a great chance for every kid to expand their knowledge about New Zealand and impress family and friends with all "discovered and never knew before" amazing facts.

New Zealand is an island
country surrounded by the
South Pacific Ocean and lies to
the Southeast of Australia.

There are two main islands in
New Zealand and 700 smaller
ones. The main islands are
called the North Island and
the South Island.

New Zealand stands part of
the Pacific Ring of Fire.

New Zealand is the 3rd closest
country to Antarctica, only after
Chile and Argentina.

Around one-third of the country is protected national parkland and marine reserves.

Māori were the first inhabitants of Aotearoa, New Zealand, guided by Kupe, the great navigator.

The first settlers probably arrived from Polynesia between 1200 and 1300 AD. They discovered New Zealand as they explored the Pacific, navigating by the ocean currents, winds, and stars.

In 1642, Dutch explorer and navigator Abel Tasman set out on a mission to explore the southern Pacific Ocean as an agent of the Dutch East India Company, and encountered the territories currently known as New Zealand, Tonga, and Fiji.

The mapmakers at the Dutch East India Company decided to call Tasman's new find "Nieuw Zeeland" after a province of the Netherlands. Zeeland translates as "sea land.

Then after 127 years, the Englishman Captain James Cook arrived there in 1769 on the first of 3 voyages. European whalers and sealers then started visiting regularly, followed by traders.

New Zealand became an independent Dominion in 1907.

National founder of New Zealand is James Busby.

National day of New Zealand is 6th February.

National Flag is "The Flag of New Zealand."

The Flag was adopted on 24 March 1902.

New Zealand's national flag's design is a defaced British Blue Ensign and has the national flag of Great Britain at the canton. The flag is rectangular in shape with 1:2 proportion and with three colors: red, blue, and white. The Union Jack at the canton represents the close relationship between New Zealand and the United Kingdom, as well as New Zealand's past as a colony of Great Britain. The Southern Cross shows the South Pacific Ocean location of the country and blue represents the sky and the sea.

Its design represents New Zealand's history as a bicultural nation.

It features four shields. The first quarter of the shield portrays four stars representing the Southern Cross, the second quarter shows a fleece which represents the farming industry, the wheat sheaf in the third quarter is a tribute to the agricultural industry and the last, (fourth) quarter with the crossed hammers recognizes the mining industry. The three ships in the center of the shield symbolize the sea trade. On left side there is a European female figure holding the New Zealand flag and, on the right, there is a Maori Chieftain holding a taiaha. A Crown represents New Zealand's status as a constitutional monarchy.

National Anthem is "God Save the Queen" and God Defend New Zealand."

God Save the Queen was adopted in 1841 and God Defend New Zealand was adopted in 1977.

National bird of New Zealand is Kiwi.

Kiwi and Moa are the most famous birds indigenous to New Zealand. Unfortunately, Moa was hunted to extinction in late 16th century.

Moa birds were around 3 m tall when standing and weighting over 200 kg.

New Zealand has a very diverse bird population. There are many bird species to find in the country, particularly different species of parrots.

The only land mammals native to NZ are bats. The rest were introduced by Maoris and Europeans.

National flower of New Zealand
is Kōwhai.

National tree of New Zealand is
Silver Fern.

There is no official national dish of New Zealand. But pie is widely regarded as a New Zealand culinary icon and staple. It comes pippin' hot with crispy pastry and chock full of a glorious savory filling.

National sports of New Zealand is Rugby.

New Zealand managed to win the Rugby World Cup 3 times.

The most popular sports to play in New Zealand are football, cricket, golf, and netball.

The official national dance of New Zealand is not declared but Haka is most popular dance in NZ, and it is a ceremonial dance in Māori culture.

New Zealand sports teams' practice of performing a haka before their international matches has made the haka more widely known around the world.

National color of New Zealand is Black.

National drink of New Zealand is Lemon & Paeroa.

Lemon & Paeroa, also known as L&P, is a sweet soft drink manufactured in New Zealand.

Created in 1907, it was traditionally made by combining lemon juice with carbonated mineral water from the town of Paeroa but is now owned and manufactured by multi-national Coca-Cola.

National monument of New Zealand is National War Memorial.

Taonga pūoro are the traditional musical instruments of the Māori people of New Zealand.

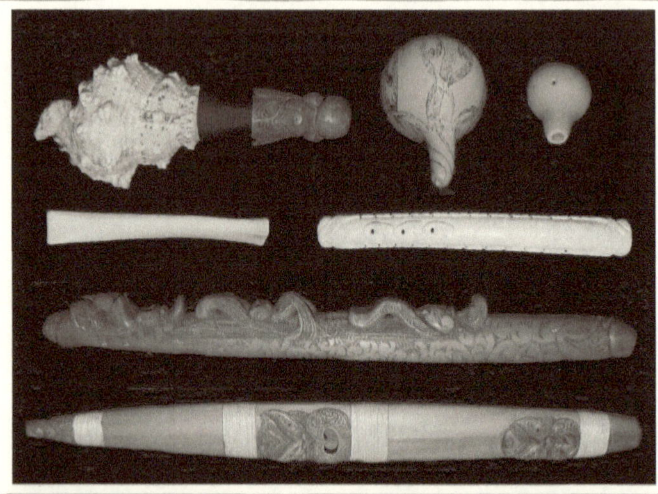

National currency of New Zealand is "New Zealand dollar."

National mausoleum of New Zealand is Pukeahu National War Memorial Park.

English is the predominant language in New Zealand, spoken by 95.4% of the population.

New Zealand has **three official languages:** English, Maori and New Zealand Sign Language.

Literacy rate of New Zealand is 100%.

The Capital of New Zealand is **Wellington**.

Wellington is the **southernmost capital** in the **world**.

Wellington has been the capital of New Zealand since 1865.

New Zealand's first capital city was **Old Russell.**

In addition to governmental institutions, Wellington accommodates several of the nation's largest and oldest cultural institutions, such as the National Archives, the National Library, New Zealand's national museum and numerous theaters.

New Zealand is one of the countries where the largest and most populous city is not the capital. The biggest city in New Zealand is Auckland while the capital is Wellington. They are both located on the North Island.

Kiwi has many meanings in NZ. Kiwi typically refers to the local people of New Zealand. A kiwifruit is a food. A kiwi bird is a famous flightless bird.

In 1893, New Zealand became the first nation to grant women the right to vote.

Due to its geographical position and shape, New Zealand experiences maritime climate.
55. Aoraki / Mount Cook is the highest mountain in New Zealand. It is 3,724 meters (12,218 feet) high. It sits in the Southern Alps.

Aoraki / Mount Cook was originally named by Māori people as "Aoraki", which means "Cloud Piercer".

The lowest point of New Zealand is Taieri Plains which is 2 meters below sea level.

New Zealand's Blue Lake, located in Nelson Lakes National Park, has the clearest water in the world.

New Zealand's Ninety Mile Beach is 90 kilometers long.

About one third of the country is protected national park.

New Zealand is home to over 400 public and private golf courses.

With more than 400, New Zealand has more golf courses per capita than anywhere else in the world.

The heaviest insect in the world is New Zealand's Weta Bug.

Out of all the population of New Zealand, only 5% are humans. The rest 95% inhabitants are animals.

There are more species of penguins native to New Zealand than to any other country.

It's a common misconception that New Zealand has no snakes, but it's not the truth. Marine snakes, or sea snakes, are seen regularly in the waters around northern New Zealand.

50% of all dolphins and whales are found in New Zealand.

Hector's dolphins are the smallest and rarest marine dolphins in the world. They are found only in the shallow coastal waters along western shores of New Zealand's North Island.

Hector's dolphin was named after Sir James Hector (1834–1907), who was the curator of the Colonial Museum in Wellington.

The North Island of New
Zealand has a place named
"**Taumatawhakatangihangakoa
uauotamateaturipukakapikima
ungahoronukupokaiwhenuakit
anatahu** "

This place holds the Guinness
World Record for longest place
name with 85 characters and
is in the township of
Porangahau.

The population of **New Zealand** is **4,935,793** as of Tuesday, May 30, 2023.

There are more vending machines in Japan than there are people in New Zealand.

New Zealand's Milford Sound was named the world's top travel destination in 2008, based on an international survey by TripAdvisor.

Jogging was first pioneered by coach Arthur Lydiard at the beginning of the 1960s, in New Zealand.

Colin Murdoch developed the first **disposable syringe** in 1956. Until that point, syringes were reused and that was causing a serious issue because infections were spreading from one patient to another using the reused syringes.

New Zealanders were the first to come up with the extreme sport **Bungee Jumping.**

David Strang of Invercargill, a New Zealander invented and **patented instant coffee in 1890.**

In 1954 William Hamilton managed to create the first **jet boat** that would leave out the propeller. It was a historic moment in the history of New Zealand, as the Hamilton Jet brand became a leader in the market.

Norma McCulloh invented the **vacuum freezing pump**, a cheap alternative for the everyday household in freezing food using plastic bags without leaving in any air bubbles.

Ernest Rutherford was a New Zealand physicist who is known as the father of nuclear physics.

The **Rutherford Medal** is the most prestigious award offered by the Royal Society of New Zealand, consisting of a medal and prize of $100,000.

Sir Edmund Hillary was a remarkable New Zealand mountaineer and explorer who gained worldwide fame for being the first person, along with Tenzing Norgay, to successfully summit Mount Everest.

He received the Knight Commander of the Order of the British Empire (KBE) from Queen Elizabeth II, becoming Sir Edmund Hillary. He also received the Order of New Zealand, the highest honor in New Zealand, among many other awards.

Zorbing, also known as globe-riding or sphereing, was invented by New Zealanders David and Andrew Akers in the 1990s. It involves rolling down a hill inside a large, transparent inflatable ball. This exhilarating activity has gained popularity worldwide as a recreational sport.

Bill Gallagher created electric fence that is used in prisons, warehouses, government buildings, and several other locations where security is important.

Bill Gallagher's initial device was created by using the car ignition trembler coil set and was geared towards keeping horses from scratching his car.

Developed by New Zealand engineer Arthur Bishop in the 1950s, the anti-roll bar is a component that reduces body roll in vehicles during cornering. It has become a standard feature in most modern automobiles, enhancing stability and safety on the road.

New Zealand ranks 8th among the **top dairy producers** in the world.

Over past 20 years **Fergburger** is a hamburger restaurant located in Queenstown, New Zealand, which specializes in gourmet hamburgers with 30 types of burgers featured on their menu, from common ones to more exotic.

New Zealanders eat **more ice cream** than any other nation on the planet: a whopping 28 liters per person per year.

New Zealand produces 100 kg of butter and 65 kg of cheese each year per person.

New Zealand doesn't have the most sheep in the world, but it has one of the world's highest ratios of sheep per capita. There are 5 times more sheep than people in New Zealand.

New Zealand is the 14th largest beef producer in the world and the 5th largest beef exporter.

Manuka honey is produced by bees foraging on the flowers of the Manuka tree, a very special tree that only grows in New Zealand. It is found that Manuka honey has bioactive healing properties and effective at boosting the body's immune system, healing wounds, treating skin infections, sore throats and digestive problems and many other things.

The **Pohutukawa tree** is also known as a New Zealand Christmas tree due to the red blooms on its branches in December.

All tv promotion is banned in New Zealand on Good Friday, Easter Sunday, ANZAC Day, and Christmas Day.

The tallest man-made structure in the Southern Hemisphere is the **Sky Tower in Auckland.**

NZ was voted the world's best country in 2007 and 2008 by Wanderlust magazine.

According to the Corruptions Perception Index, New Zealand is the least corrupt nation in the world, tied with Denmark.

Almost all personal financial transactions in New Zealand are done with a card. Cash is used very rarely.

According to the **Guinness Book of Records**, the steepest street in the world is located on the South Island of New Zealand and is **Baldwin Street**, with a **slope of 19 degrees**.

The **driest city** in New Zealand is **Christchurch**.

The **wettest city** in New Zealand is **Wellington**.

Due to its geographical position and shape, New Zealand experiences **maritime climate**.

New Zealand is home to over **400 public and private** golf courses.

New Zealand is the second highest number of courses per capita of any country in the world.

New Zealand is the only country legally permitted to have images connected to the **Hobbits on its currency**.

Ships navigating in New Zealand water has a famous dolphin as a guide.

Pelorus Jack was a Risso's dolphin ,that was famous for meeting and escorting ships through a stretch of water in Cook Strait, New Zealand.

Some of the accomplishments of NASA's space program are the result of the efforts of astrophysicist **Dr William Pickering,** who is a Kiwi.

New Zealand ranks **ninth** among the world's longest coasts.

The oldest organized sport in
New Zealand is **cricket**.

The first referee to use
a **whistler** to stop a
match is a Kiwi.

New Zealand was the first modern-day country ever to appoint an **Official National Wizard.**

Ninety Mile Beach is actually **90 km long**.

No part of the country is more than **128km (79 miles) from the sea.**

New Zealand's North Island
ranks **14th** in the world's largest
islands.

New Zealand is among
only **three** countries in Oceania.

Gisborne is the first city on the
planet to see the sunrise every
single day.

Please check this out: Our other best-selling books for kids are-

All About **New York**: Interesting & Amazing Facts That Everyone Should Know

All About **New Jersey**: Interesting & Amazing Facts That Everyone Should Know

All About **Massachusetts**: 100+ Amazing Facts with Pictures

All About **Florida**: Interesting & Amazing Facts That Everyone Should Know

All About **California**: Interesting & Amazing Facts That Everyone Should Know

All About **Arizona**: Interesting & Amazing Facts That Everyone Should Know

**Please check this out:
Our other best-selling books for kids are-**
Ukraine: Interesting & Amazing Facts That
Everyone Should Know
Germany: Interesting & Amazing
Facts That
Everyone Should Know
Switzerland: Interesting & Amazing
Facts That
Everyone Should Know
New Zealand: Interesting & Amazing
Facts That
Everyone Should Know
Brazil: Interesting & Amazing Facts
That
Everyone Should Know
Argentina: Interesting & Amazing
Facts That
Everyone Should Know

Please check this out:
Our other best-selling books for kids are-

All About **France**: Interesting & Amazing Facts That Everyone Should Know

All About **Japan:** Interesting & Amazing Facts That Everyone Should Know

Know About Whales: Interesting & Amazing Facts That Everyone Should Know

Know About Dinosaurs: Interesting & Amazing Facts That Everyone Should Know

Know About Kangaroos: Interesting & Amazing Facts That Everyone Should Know

Please check this out:
Our other best-selling books for kids are-

Chile: Interesting & Amazing Facts That Everyone Should Know

Denmark Interesting & Amazing Facts That Everyone Should Know

All About **Canada**: Interesting & Amazing Facts That Everyone Should Know

All About **Australia**: Interesting & Amazing Facts That Everyone Should Know

All About **Italy**: Interesting & Amazing Facts That Everyone Should Know

Please check this out:
Our other best-selling books for kids are-

All About **Texas**: Interesting & Amazing Facts That Everyone Should Know

All About **Minnesota**: Interesting & Amazing Facts That Everyone Should Know

All About **Illinois**: Interesting & Amazing Facts That Everyone Should Know

All About **New Mexico**: Interesting & Amazing Facts That Everyone Should Know

Know about Sharks: Interesting & Amazing Facts That Everyone Should Know

Please check this out:
Our other best-selling books for kids are-

100 Amazing Quiz Q & A About Penguin: Never Known Before Penguin Facts

Most Popular Animal Quiz book for Kids: 100 amazing animal facts

Quiz Book for Kids: Science, History, Geography, Biology, Computer & Information Technology

English Grammar for Kids: Most Easy Way to learn English Grammar

Solar System & Space Science- Quiz for Kids: What You Know About Solar System

English Grammar Practice Book for elementary kids: 1000+ Practice Questions with Answers